BEYOND EQU

CW01020774

WOMEN AND MEN II

by Lorna Ashworth

A member of the Church of England General Synod

Published 2010 by Brexworthy Press
Manor Barn, Horsington, BA8 0ET

Copyright © Lorna Ashworth 2010
ISBN 978-0-9565834-0-6

Cover & Interior Design: Inspired Designs

INTRODUCTION
· · · · · · · · · · · · ·

'As a woman, my journey with the subject of biblical headship and the role of women within the church has been a bumpy one.'

I have toiled with the fine line of my desire to obey scripture whilst not wanting to bother trying to critically understand those 'difficult' passages; the passages that with a shallow reading suggest a sexist interpretation. My temptation has been to default to the common mindset of 'I don't see why not'. However, this approach neither constitutes a basis for biblical debate nor biblical application. If the total sum of this debate was about the social implications of gender injustice, then I would have been the first to sign up. Gender discrimination has been and still is a real issue in the world today, and one that must continue to be addressed. But with regards to this issue I have come to firmly believe that this is not about gender injustice, but about how God, in his perfect wisdom, has chosen to order His Church. For me, this has been a liberating discovery; something that goes far beyond equal rights.

Our responsibility and desire must be above all to obey God, and His living and written Word. Therefore it is my earnest desire that this paper will provide an accessible groundwork for introducing the subject to those who have not yet had the opportunity to think through the issues surrounding this debate, and to encourage a biblical approach whilst doing so.

This paper will start by looking at the framework in which the debate needs to be set; that is, in the nature and character of God himself as expressed within the Godhead. This will be followed by how God's relationship ideal is ordained in His creation and how that ideal was corrupted by the Fall. With that framework in place, I will look at biblical headship with regards to the husband/wife role and variations of Church Order within the Evangelical position. Then I will go on to view those of the Anglo-Catholic and Egalitarian positions. Before concluding I have looked at a few of the many questions people ask in relation to women in the Bible.

May we unashamedly embrace integrity and faithfulness in handling difficult biblical passages (whatever the subject) and have the willingness to obey the Word of God even when it grinds in the face of secular culture.

IN THE BEGINNING

· · · · · · · · · · · · · ·

The Godhead

The article in Third Way magazine shouts out big and bold, 'HOW UNLIKE GOD. If women, no less than men, are made in the image of their creator, how come they are still less than equal?'[1]

The writer goes on, unfortunately, to fuel the misunderstanding that somehow difference in function equates difference in value, i.e. that women are treated as inferior to men if not granted the same opportunities within the church. This argument is weak and highly offensive when set against the revealed nature and character of God. Why? Because if this proposed principle is true, then we serve a God who has 'institutionalised' discrimination within the Godhead.

Within the Godhead the parallel of equality and differing function exist in perfect unity. The members of the Godhead are equal in glory but unequal in role. The Father leads, the Son submits to the Father, and the Holy Spirit submits to both the Son and the Father. Nowhere in scripture do we see these roles reversed.

[1] Jane Shaw *Third Way* p.24, vol.24, no.8 November 2001

'Now I want you to realise that the head of every man is Christ, and the head of the woman is man, and the head of Christ is God.'

1 Corinthians ch.11 v.3

'When he has done this, then the Son himself will be made subject to him who put everything under him, so that God may be all in all.'

1 Corinthians ch.15 v.28

The concept of headship and submission never had a beginning point. 'It has always existed in the eternal nature of God Himself.'[2] This authority has nothing to do with value, gifts or ability. It is the way that God is in relation to Himself and will be forever. Raymond C. Ortlund Jr explains that as it is God's nature to exist in this way, 'Christians, of all people, have a reason to live with paradox … if our Creator exists in this manner, should we be surprised and offended if His creaturely analogue on earth exists in paradoxical form?'[3]

If one truly believes that difference in role makes one party inferior to the other, then we are in a serious spot of bother! If Jesus is inferior to God the Father due to His role within the Godhead not only would He be guilty in claiming equality with God[4], but doubt is cast upon our very salvation. Could an inferior member of the Godhead provide an atoning substitute for our sin?[5] Where does this leave the Holy Spirit? Presumably worse off than the Son!

---

[2] Ibid p.47

[3] Raymond C. Ortlund Jr., Recovering Biblical Manhood & Womanhood, ch. 3 p.103, Crossway Books, Wheaton, Illinois 1991

[4] John chs 5 v.18, 8 v.58, & 14 v.7 etc.

[5] Hebrews ch.1 vv.1-4 & Revelation ch.5 v.9

The model of relationship presented to us within the Godhead provides a beautiful framework which then extends into His creation.

'Who, being in very nature God, did not consider equality with God something to be grasped, but made himself nothing, taking the very nature of a servant, being made in human likeness. And being found in appearance as a man, he humbled himself and became obedient to death – even death on a cross!'

Philippians ch.2 vv.6-8

The Created Order

The Bible clearly teaches that men and women are created equally in the image of God.[6]

The Holy Spirit was given to both at Pentecost and both are baptised into the body of Christ. We equally receive spiritual gifts for use in the life of the Church. Together, male and female, we are created for filial relationship with God, and are intended to express this family likeness in righteousness. It is in God's image that we find the foundation for human dignity and intrinsic worth.[7] Shall we therefore conclude that uniformity should span into our role responsibilities? I would argue no. Instead we see the equality and role differentiation paradox introduced into the male-female relationship as they reflect the image of God together at no cost to individual self worth.

[6] Genesis ch.1 vv.26-27, Acts ch.2 vv.17-18 & 41, 1 Corinthians ch.12 vv.7 & 11, Galatians ch.3 v.28, 1 Peter ch.4 v.10

[7] New Dictionary of Theology, Inter-Varsity Press, p.329, Leicester, England 1988

[8]Despite the equality outlined above, there are a number of indicators in the Genesis account which point to a differentiation in roles for Adam and Eve. God created male and female in His image equally, but He also instructed the male to lead and the female as his helper (see Genesis ch.2 v.18).

Several indicators of male headship can be seen.

- 1 Timothy ch.2 v.13 explicitly makes the point that man is created first and then woman.

- Eve is created to be Adam's 'helper'. Whilst this role should not be understood in a way that makes it degrading or demeaning, the obvious point should not be ignored that it suggests a 'supportive' role. God put Adam in the garden 'to work it and take care of it' (Genesis ch. 2 v.15), and gave him instruction how to live under God's command (vv.16-17), Eve is then created to help him in this role.

- The fact that Adam names Eve is a clear sign of authority. Whilst it is Eve alone who is suitable for Adam (unlike all the animals), nonetheless it is to Adam that God gives the responsibility of naming her, just as he has named the animals. He chooses the generic term 'woman' because she has come from 'man' (v.23) and then later he 'named his wife Eve, because she would become the mother of all the living' (ch.3 v.20).

[8] The following section up to ' The Fall ' is with permission based on Women Bishops in the Church of England, pp.7-8, A study booklet by Moulton Parish Church

- Returning to ch.2 v.24, when the writer applies this first husband-wife relationship to all future ones he says, 'For this reason a man will leave his father and mother, ...' not, 'a woman will leave her father and mother, ...' nor even 'man and woman will leave their fathers and mothers ...'. It is the man who initiates the new household.

For some people, the very word 'helper' sounds derogatory or demeaning. But it should be noted that there is no such connotation in Genesis ch.2. Indeed, everything about Eve is positive; she is the solution to the man's aloneness, and she is suitable for him (v.18); Adam responds with great delight when he sees her (v.23); and the relationship between Adam and Eve becomes the blueprint for all future marriages (v.24). Furthermore, in the majority of instances in which the word 'helper' is used in the Bible, it refers to God himself, and can thus hardly be considered derogatory.

Thus the picture from Genesis chs 1-3 is of man and woman created spiritually equal in the image of God, and given different and complementary roles with the woman helping the man to lead.

The Fall

We all know that Eve took the first bite in Genesis chapter 3!

But here it is important to appreciate the two obvious consequences with regard to relationships.

First to note is the fact that Adam but not Eve, is held accountable for the Fall since he was the one with primary responsibility. So in ch.3 v.9 it is Adam that is summoned before God. Rather than exercising godly leadership he became a passive observer, abdicating his role, and henceforth it is Adam who becomes known as the one through whom sin entered the world.

'Like Adam, they have broken the covenant – they were unfaithful to me there.'

Hosea ch.6 v.7

'Therefore, just as sin entered the world through one man..., For if the many died by the trespass of the one man, ... For if, by the trespass of the one man, death reigned through that one man, ...'

Romans ch.5 vv.12, 15 & 17

'For as in Adam all die, so in Christ all will be made alive.'

1 Corinthians ch.15 v.22

Second, the resulting judgement pronounced on the woman introduced a tension into the relationship that had never been intended. 'Your desire will be for your husband, and he will rule over you;' (Genesis ch.3 v.16b).[9]

---

[9] 'rule over you' could mean, he will practice godly leadership over ungodly influence, or he will give in to his own sin and dominate in an ungodly manner.

In other words, 'differentiated roles were corrupted, not created by the Fall'.[10] 'The pattern established prior to the fall was a hierarchy of roles characterised by unity and oneness. The judgement would work against, rather than contribute to this original created order and unity.'[11]

It follows that we cannot go on ascribing male domination as biblical doctrine where clearly it is a personal moral failure and an indulgence of sin.

[10] John Piper, Recovering Biblical Manhood & Womanhood, p.35 Crossway Books, Wheaton, Illinois 1991

[11] Mary A. Kassian, Women, Creation and the Fall, p.26 Crossway Books, Westchester, Illinois 1990

BIBLICAL HEADSHIP

· · · · · · · · · · · · ·

The Framework

Believers whose identity is found in Christ Jesus have a certain privilege and responsibility to live as those redeemed by God.

This means we should seek to live out our lives according to His Word. In terms of this debate, when moving on from the teaching of Genesis to the Bible as a whole, the framework God has provided for this task can be seen.

Though some people would distort it, Jesus is seen to reinstate it; likewise the Apostle Paul reaffirms it during the establishment of the early Church. It is through this framework (referred to as 'biblical headship') that we ourselves need to approach those biblical texts we find so hard to swallow. With this background in place we turn now to see its application first in the husband wife relationship and secondly within the variations of church order found in the Evangelical position.

Husband / Wife Relationship

It is at this point we come to one of those passages some people deem as problematic. I for one find it beautiful, liberating and humbling, all at the same time!

'Wives, submit to your husbands as to the Lord. For the husband is the head of the wife as Christ is the head of the church, his body, of which he is the Saviour. Now as the church submits to Christ, so also wives should submit to their husbands in everything. Husbands, love your wives, just as Christ loved the church and gave himself up for her to make her holy, cleansing her by the washing with water through the word, and to present her to himself as a radiant church, without stain or wrinkle or any other blemish, but holy and blameless. In this same way, husbands ought to love their wives as their own bodies. He who loves his wife loves himself. After all, no one ever hated his own body, but he feeds and cares for it, just as Christ does the church – for we are members of his body. For this reason a man will leave his father and mother and be united to his wife, and the two will become one flesh. This is a profound mystery – but I am talking about Christ and the church. However, each one of you also must love his wife as he loves himself, and the wife must respect her husband.'

Ephesians ch.5 vv.22-33

The first thing that strikes me about this passage is that it has more to do with the role of men than the role of women. Second, it makes me glad that I'm not a man! So much time is wasted on the very first line that we end up distorting the profundity of what is being said. It is here that we are presented with God's expectations of a man living rightly under God's loving rule, and it is without a doubt a high calling. He is to love his wife in every way that Christ loves His Church.

14

It is passionate and it is sacrificial. 'The husband takes the lead, but not in an overbearing or selfish way. Like Christ dying for His Church, his sole concern is to love his wife, and lay down his life for her. The wife follows this lead and supports her husband in it. She gladly submits, as she does to Christ – not in menial servitude and oppressed silence, but in love and respect and unity. The marriage grows to joyous levels of intimacy and strength.'[12] I am personally humbled by the privilege of my own calling under God, as a married woman to submit to such love, and as women in general, we need to pray for men to get busy loving their wives in this Christ-like manner. Without God's strength, 'these roles can quickly degenerate into chauvinism, feminism, selfishness and arguing.'[13]

> *'Our culture has become so preoccupied with asserting our personal rights that even Christians have forgotten that greatness in the Kingdom of God is measured by servanthood.'[14]*

What a shame it is that submission is so misunderstood, because this biblical pattern is a source of incredible joy, fulfilment and contentment.

---

[12] Bryson Smith, Walk This Way – Ephesians, p. 54, Mathias Media 1996, 2001
[13] Ibid
[14] Ibid

Variations of Church Order within the Evangelical position

'I want men everywhere to lift up holy hands in prayer, without anger or disputing. I also want women to dress modestly, with decency and propriety, not with braided hair or gold or pearls or expensive clothes, but with good deeds, appropriate for women who profess to worship God. A woman should learn in quietness and full submission. I do not permit a woman to teach or to have authority over a man; she must be silent. For Adam was formed first, then Eve. And Adam was not the one deceived; it was the woman who was deceived and became a sinner. But women will be saved through child bearing – if they continue in faith, love and holiness with propriety.'

1 Timothy ch.2 vv.8-15

Though all Evangelicals have a similar high regard for scripture, some have differences of opinion regarding this subject. For the sake of simplicity and space, I have chosen to use only one Bible passage.

First there are those who do not believe scripture prohibits women from the roles of presbyter and bishop. Secondly, there are differences amongst Evangelicals with regards to the application of biblical headship within church order. These differences are arrived at mainly through the interpretation of the above passage and are explained below. For lack of a better description, I have termed them Churches A, B, and C. The first two are most common and the third is quite rare.

Church A

Those holding this position, support biblical headship and would not support the ordination of women as deacons, priests or bishops nor would they have female lay readers.

Women may or may not read the Bible in a mixed assembly of men and women. Women will however be allowed to teach Sunday School and have a ministry amongst other women.

These churches could be called 'literalist' when it comes to the interpretation of 1 Timothy ch.2 vv.11-15.

Church B

Those holding this position would not support women as bishops or priests, but would usually support women deacons. They would also have female lay readers.

Women would preach in church, though probably not on a regular basis, and they would do so with the understanding that the male presbyter is seen as the one with God-given authority.

Their view of this passage places a greater emphasis on discerning between what is cultural and what is universal. Beginning with verses 8-10, the cultural element identified is that men may or may not lift up their hands while praying. The expression of prayer is culturally different and may change with time. Secondly, when women dress up (and there is no prohibition to this as some suggest) they should do so in a modest way appropriate to that culture.

The unchanging universal principle applied is that as men pray, they do so in holiness of heart, free from the things that hinder them such as anger and disputing. For women, they should always seek to adorn themselves with a spiritual beauty that comes from knowing God.

Finally, when coming to verses 11 and those following, we see presented two sets of exact opposites. Authority versus submission and teaching versus silence. The question continues, what is cultural and what is universal? Those in this category would maintain that authority versus submission is to be retained as universal and teaching versus silence as cultural. As a result women may teach but in the context that they are not acting in the role of 'elder' in the church. The role of elder is touched on below.

The Church B model is the position that I have personally arrived at.

Church C

Those holding this position would say that women could be deacons and priests but not bishops.

This view is not widely held in evangelical circles and is more difficult to defend scripturally, however it is worth mentioning. In the New Testament there are two named church 'offices'; that of 'elder' and that of 'deacon'. The elder has other names ascribed to him which are interchangeable (such as Pastor/Overseer/Bishop).

As the churches grew in number in the first and second centuries, an overseeing role developed that eventually came to be described as the bishop. The bishop who really was an elder was simply 'consecrated' or set apart for a different job and initially not seen to be someone of higher rank. However Bishops are now seen to have a certain level of authority and hence some see this as the focal point not only of unity but of authority, therefore it follows that women cannot be bishops because they are the ones with authority, but they can be deacons or priests.

So then, using the models of Church A and Church B, how would a practical outworking of biblical headship look in the running of the Church of England?

First of all, theological colleges would be full of both men and women seeking to be equipped for full or part-time ministry. Some women and men would be training specifically for the diaconate, others for youth ministry or other types of ministry. Obviously there would also be men training for the priesthood.

Women could go on to work within churches where, as part of a team, they would have a specific ministry amongst women, children or young people. In this they may or may not be permitted to preach to mixed congregations, depending on the specific view of the incumbent (see my points made under 'variations of church order').

These women would open up a fresh dynamic of ministry as part of a team. They would experience the joy of working with the male incumbent who acknowledges their gifts and provides the support necessary for the flourishing of that ministry within the framework that God has designed.

Although not an ordained deacon myself, my personal experience reflects something of the picture presented above, as does that of many other women I know. To give you an idea, my brief resume includes these. 'Overseas ministry projects' - first as a teenager on a building project in Poland and later in Jamaica and Malawi. 'Wider church involvement' - enjoying (yes enjoying) serving on the PCC, Deanery, Diocesan and General Synods. 'Local church involvement' - over 15 years of youth ministry both at church and in co-leading a CYFA camp, leading two home groups and co-ordinating the home group ministry, planting a new afternoon family service in my parish church with my husband where I preach quite regularly. 'Local community' - using puppets to teach the Bible in local schools, and finally, just being a mum on the sidelines of the rugby pitch every weekend enjoying the company of other parents and developing lovely friendships! I could go on, but suffice to say that there are many other opportunities for women to serve in team ministry as an ordained deacon, employed lay minister or volunteer, as in my situation.

This pattern, described in a very basic way is one that many evangelical churches are seeking to emulate. That is, to provide more opportunities for the essential ministry of women within churches whilst retaining biblical integrity. Some might suggest that this type of ministry is insulting and restrictive to women, but as Carrie Sandom puts it, 'To say that ministry to women is restrictive and does not constitute a full ministry is to deny women their worth and demonstrates a covert misogyny that I abhor'.[15]

Although I have very frugally highlighted differences in how some evangelical churches operate, what should be at the fore is that life in God's creation was intended to be lived with freedom in the pattern He set out for us. Due to the Fall, this journey was never going to be smooth; this however does not excuse us from pursuing obedience to God's Word. With God's help it is our privilege to mirror the redeemed community of God and one of the ways that this is reflected is how we treat each other.[16] This is not some lofty ideal; this is meant to be reality.

---

[15] Carrie Sandom, 'Desiring what is true or defending desire?' p. 7 Reform's presentation to the Rochester Commission concerning Women in the Episcopate, Reform 2001

[16] Mike Ovey, 'Desiring what is true or defending desire?' p. 4, presentation to the Rochester Commission concerning Women in the Episcopate, Reform 2001

Anglo-Catholic position

In summary, their opposition results from the belief in sacramental assurance.

Consecrated Women? A Contribution to the Women Bishops Debate provides a thorough and comprehensive look at the Anglo-Catholic position.[17] Just as there are varying positions held by evangelicals there are also variances within the Anglo-Catholic tradition, each with their own emphasis. This small section will only provide a general summary.

Anglo-Catholics differ with Evangelicals as to the precise significance of holy orders and hence their immutability. That is to say because a presbyter or bishop has an iconographic function as a representative of the incarnate Christ, particularly at the celebration of the Eucharist, it follows therefore that he must be male. As a result there is serious doubt as to whether the process of Ordination to the office of Priest or Bishop is even possible where the person being ordained is a woman. This in turn raises doubts as to whether the sacramental functions that she performs in this office are according to the purposes of Jesus Christ and hence to their sacramental validity. In other words any purported sacraments ministered by them would be utterly null and totally void of grace to affect salvation.

---

[17] Consecrated Women? A Contribution to the Women Bishops Debate, Jonathan Baker (ed), Canterbury Press, Norwich, 2004

Evangelicals likewise take Holy Communion very seriously, but would have a different emphasis on the means by which God works through the use of this sacrament. In addition, they would generally take the view that scripture seems to give no explicit instructions as to whether the person presiding is lay or ordained, male or female. However, for the sake of order it will usually be ordained clergy. Specifically, in the Church of England, it can only be administered by a presbyter assisted by those duly selected.

The Egalitarian Position

> *The driving force behind the proponents for the consecration of women as bishops is quite simply gender justice.*

For them, the Church is actively legislating for gender discrimination, and until such time as women are fully welcomed into the threefold order of ministry (deacons, priests and bishops), the Church continues to enshrine this dated and unacceptable ideology. It is an anathema and an embarrassment to think otherwise.

With this in mind the press has reported that, 'The Church needs to catch up with Jesus Christ',[18] and that we will see greater wholeness and reconciliation 'when the Church recognises the full humanity of women'.[19]

---

[18] Christina Rees, The Church of England Newspaper, 20 February 2003
[19] Ibid

We are told as well that, the Church of England is looked upon with bemusement by the outside world.

Furthermore, they most likely perceive it to be misogynist and that until this situation is properly rectified, the Gospel work in England is hindered.

This debate, as with any in the Church, needs to stay grounded in scripture and we need to be clear about the terminology we are using. As mentioned earlier, the evangelical position holds firmly to the equality of men and women both created in the image of God. However, what I believe is being referred to as 'equality' by the egalitarians is in fact 'uniformity'; two very different things. Equality has to do with our intrinsic worth whereas uniformity concerns our sameness. To equate personal value with our role is insulting. This continual appeal for uniformity denies men and women the richness found in our God-given distinctiveness; any attempt to use the Bible to support this position is untenable. The classic example of this error is found in the misuse of Galatians ch.3 v.28, the pivotal text used as a motto for uniformity.

'There is neither Jew nor Greek, slave nor free, male nor female, for you are all one in Christ Jesus.'

This passage, when put in context with the rest of the letter, very clearly teaches that the grace of Jesus Christ is available to everyone who comes to him; we are all on an equal footing in Christ.

It is not conditional to our ethnicity, position in life or gender. To use this verse to say that as we are equal in Christ any distinctions are nullified is irresponsible hermeneutics.

Yet, in spite of this error, it is the Traditionalists that are accused by some of abandoning critical scholarship for 'crude interpretations of scripture and for an understanding of tradition that makes it frozen in a particular time rather than dynamic'.[20] The irony of this statement can be seen in the attempt to make a 'biblical' argument about St Paul leaving us with 'troubling biblical texts'. It is suggested that these texts resulted as he capitulated to the values of pagan Roman society when other churches managed for centuries to maintain a radical equality of women. Are we to conclude then, that out of fear and frustration of the culture Paul lived in, that he sidelined God's commission to him as an apostle in favour of pagan values and left us with uninspired empty words, void of the Holy Spirit? Are 'troubling biblical texts' those that annoy us? This subjective approach to scripture leads us into very dangerous waters indeed.

---

[20] Jane Shaw 'Women & the Episcopate', p.18 Affirming Catholicism journal, London 2006

One final observation by John Hunwicke with regard to the biblical approach used by the Egalitarians is that they have begun with an,

'a priori determination to have women bishops and then set about putting arguments together. "We ought to have women bishops because they had them in the New Testament and the New Testament is normative; and if they didn't have them then they were wrong and we should have them now because we all know so much better" is not an argument in favour of the innovation. It is a contradiction upon which it would be very unwise to act'.[21]

It seems that for some people one can be dismissive about scripture if limited value is ascribed to it.

---

[21] John Hunwicke, Consecrated Women? A Comparison, p.2 Forward in Faith, London 2005

SOME COMMONLY ASKED QUESTIONS
· · · · · · · · · · · · ·

What about Deborah in the Old Testament?
(see Judges ch.4)

Deborah is my hero! What a lady. She was courageous, an example of faith and of godly wisdom. She lived during the dark period of the Judges when, 'In those days Israel had no king; everyone did as he saw fit' (Judges ch.21 v.25). She was a prophetess and a judge, but this fact does not overturn the role of women in relation to the leadership of God's people. Prophecy came to both men and women and is not about oversight or church order.

She held court under a tree where the people of Israel came to her for disputes to be settled. She did not act as a presbyter and is the only judge in the book of Judges not to have a military function.[22] When the word of the Lord came to Deborah concerning battle, He commanded that Barak lead the way (v.6).

---

[22] Schreiner, 'The Valuable Ministries of Women in the Context of Male Leadership', in Piper and Grudem, Recovering Biblical Manhood and Womanhood, p.216 Crossway Books, Illinois 1991

Due to his cowardice he would not go to battle without her and as a result she announced a word of rebuke on him, implying that he should not have insisted that she go to battle with him.[23] She seems to have seen limits to the kind of leadership she should exercise.[24]

What about the extraordinary role of the women at the tomb?
(see Matthew ch.28, Mark ch.16, Luke ch.24 & John ch.20)

First century Judaism did not accept the trustworthiness of women as witnesses, and their witness failed to impress the disciples initially! (See Luke ch.24 v.11.) How wonderful then that God decided that women should be the first witnesses to the resurrection of Jesus. Once again however, there is no proof in scripture that because of this event, biblical headship is reversed.

As will be seen in the next section, Jesus acted in a counter-cultural way and rightly so! He was correcting the mistreatment and marginalisation of women and demonstrating the truth we are told in Galatians ch.3 v.28. The women joyously were the first to share the good news of Jesus just as all men and women are commanded to do in the Great Commission (Matthew ch.28 vv.18-20). This does not amount to uniformity across the board.

[23] Grudem, Evangelical Feminism and Biblical Truth – an analysis of 118 disputed questions, p.132 IVP, Leicester, 2004
[24] James Rushton ed., Twenty Questions on Women's Ordination Answered, p.91 the Association for Apostolic Ministry p.9

Jesus and women in the early church?

Jesus' attitude towards women was revolutionary. 'He treated them as equals and co-heirs in the Gospel. He passed on this attitude to the apostles, for in the New Testament churches, women played a vital role, and their worth and contribution were not questioned.'[25] These women clearly used their gifts but within the recognised headship structure as the following examples show.

Priscilla

Priscilla and Aquila together had a wonderful ministry of teaching and encouragement. While in Ephesus they heard Apollos speaking in the synagogue. We are told that when they heard him, 'they invited him to their home and explained to him the way of God more adequately' (Acts ch.18 v.26). This was not a congregational setting in a public place, but a private, informal, shared act of discipleship. A few verses later it is Apollos who is once again found publicly teaching the Scriptures.

[25] Mary A. Kassian, Women, Creation and the Fall, p.87 Crossway Books, Illinois, 1990

Phoebe

Paul commends Phoebe, a servant (deacon) of the church in Cenchrea (Romans ch.16 v.1). She had been a great help to Paul and some would say that as she is called a deacon it follows that women should be leaders in the church. One important point to remember however is that it is 'elders' who are given the roles of leaders and teachers in the New Testament, not 'deacons'.

Junias / Juni - see Romans ch.16 v.7

'Greet Andronicus and Junias, my relatives who have been in prison with me. They are outstanding among the apostles, and they were in Christ before I was.'

It is impossible to claim this name as either male or female and hence erroneous to say emphatically that a woman was referred to as an apostle thus setting a precedent for women church leaders. It could very well have been a man. In addition, Grudem significantly explains that the phrase, 'outstanding or well known among' the apostles is no longer relevant in the light of recent scholarship. Since 2001, after an extensively researched technical article, the meaning 'well known to' received strong support, with significant evidence from extra biblical Greek.[26] In other words, these outstanding people, were not apostles, but known to them.

---

[26] Grudem p.224

Who are we to hinder someone God has called?

'While God does not want women to bury their talents or waste their gifts, it is wrong to misappropriate scripture to accommodate the way in which we think those gifts should be exercised.'[27]

In other words if we believe God has a specific order in how to run his church, He would not contradict that by 'calling' someone to do otherwise. He would not call someone to disobey His Word. The person may of course be very godly and sincere, but our decisions cannot be based on subjective experience.

Slavery

There is an argument which suggests that just as the Church finally got around to acknowledging that slavery was wrong, they must also recognise that their treatment of women is wrong. But surely this comparison is misguided.

Slavery is an abuse of human dignity that came after the Fall. It was not instituted by God, and models nothing of the character and nature of God. It is true to say that Christians in the past have used the Bible to condone slavery but that does not mean that it endorses slavery. To the contrary! 1 Timothy ch.1 v.10 states that the law is made '…for slave traders and liars and perjurers – and for whatever else is contrary to the sound doctrine …'.

---

[27] Kassian p.89

To say that because the Bible gave guidelines on how Christians, whether they are a slave or master, should treat each other in Christ is the same as endorsing slavery, is once again irresponsible handling of scripture.[28]

What about women in secular leadership?

If women are, in certain circumstances, better qualified and better able to lead in secular society, why should restrictions be imposed on them in the church?

The answer comes down to obedience to scripture which has clearly given commands regarding male leadership in the home and in the church. Evangelicals do not argue that women fail to have the ability or skill to lead churches, but in this matter, God in His wisdom has set boundaries which we willingly obey.

In marriage and in the Church there are covenant relationships in place (husband and wife, Christ and His people) whereas in the secular workplace they are absent. This means that a woman is free to exercise authority over men (unless of course she is working with her husband). Ephesians ch.5 v.22 encourages wives to submit to their husbands and not to every man they know! Hebrews ch.13 v.17 encourages all Christians (not just women) to submit to their church leaders.

---

[28] 1 Corinthians ch.7 v.21; Colossians ch.4 v.1; Philemon vv.15-18

Women Missionaries

Many brave and industrious single and married women have answered the call of the Great Commission in Matthew chapter 28 to 'go and make disciples of all nations' around the world. They have travelled where many have feared to tread in order to share the good news of Jesus. As a result many charities have been founded that work with street children, drug addicts, homeless adults, abused women and so forth. These pioneering efforts have also resulted in churches being planted and where there have been no male counterparts, these women have become the leader. I believe that in the case of a church plant, the women temporarily hold this position until men from that local community are raised up to lead as God intended or unless there is a spiritually mature male missionary to join the work.

At that point the woman missionary joyfully relinquishes that specific role and continues to serve in other ways. This is not an ideal situation, but necessary in order that the furtherance of the Gospel is not hindered.

*****

Perhaps in closing this section the Egalitarian or Uniformist needs to be asked whether the Bible itself is discriminatory against women, or if men are misusing the Bible to act in a discriminatory way against women? Their arguments do not mount up. I do not see that the Bible is in any way discriminatory against women. Quite the opposite. It is revolutionary, counter-cultural and liberating if they seek to live in God's world, God's way.

Those men in the Church who lovingly seek to uphold the biblical pattern of church order are not using scripture in a discriminatory manner. Uniformity is not the same as equality as seen modelled within the Godhead. There have been times, and no doubt will continue to be, when both men and women abuse scripture for their own sinful ways, and this is unacceptable.

Therefore we need to be clear about what it is we are standing up against, and I am convinced that Egalitarians are reacting against the warped abuse of scripture by men who in turn use it to dominate and suppress the humanity and gifts of women. Rightly understood and applied however, the picture is very different.

CONCLUSION

· · · · · · · · · · · · · ·

I am humbled by the beauty displayed in the coexistence of God the Father, God the Son, and God the Holy Spirit.

For me, this is where the debate begins. In contrast, the Egalitarian movement introduces a tension into this harmony and distorts the liberty of the complementary roles God has designed. I would also like to add at this point that not all supporters of women priests and women bishops are Egalitarians or Uniformists, as referred to on page 21. I have the privilege of working alongside men and women for the Gospel of Christ who disagree with me on this issue. We agree to disagree though we might try to convince each other otherwise!

Secondly, of course the world looks upon us with bemusement. How can a liberal, secular culture engage with theological or biblical matters when they have no part with the Church and no understanding of God and his Word? Should this stop us from upholding biblical truths? The answer is no, because we should not be more worried about what others think than what God thinks.

I also do not agree that an order for biblical headship prevents the Gospel from advancing. Instead, as we unashamedly bring the Gospel message to people with integrity we will see it transform lives, we will see gender discrimination eradicated whilst upholding equality and role distinction in godly paradox.

Thirdly, one of my concerns surrounding the debate is that women like myself, have had or are experiencing genuine sexist treatment in the Church; however, as a result the naïve assumption is that all dissenters are sexist. This poses problems for a few reasons.

Those people actively engaged in sexism are behaving contrary to the Word of God. As a teenager raising money to take part in an overseas mission project, I was told point blank by a man in my church that as a female I should not be going on missions and that I should not expect any money from him. More recently a male presbyter blatantly refused to share the Peace with me during the Eucharist at a Diocesan Synod meeting. My thoughts turned to concern for those under his care rather than thinking that all men or all dissenters behaved in such an un-Christ like manner. I have also received a barrage of verbal abuse from a female presbyter who was representing Women and the Church.

Likewise I wondered how her parishioners faired if they dared disagree with her on any point! I must add that not all women representing WATCH (Women and the Church) or other female presbyters treat me that way.

> *My point is that sexism is not the trademark of godly biblical headship; sexism is one of the trademarks of sin.*

Sexism cannot be attributed to all dissenters because where does that leave me? Is it possible to be sexist against myself? I find it frustrating when some women assume to 'speak' on behalf of all women by claiming that we are treated as less than human because of an apparent lack of equality. I am not that easily deceived. I stand in full confidence of my value and worth as a human being, in my equality with men before Christ, and that my value as an individual is not conditional to the role I have in the Church. Perhaps this freedom I have allows me to embrace my womanhood to a greater extent. I am free from the need to constantly assess my value in comparison to men based on what I do.

Finally, I think it is time to be entirely honest about these things. We need to stop pretending that The Church of England's General Synod is attempting to have a biblical discussion over this issue. Some are attempting a faithful biblical interpretation and others are simply trying to impose uniformity off the back of gender equality.

If this were truly a biblical debate there would be a sincere acknowledgement that both parties are loyal Anglicans. Legal provision would be offered by the proponents with the awareness that as the initiators of change, the onus is on them to assure Traditionalists, both Evangelical and Anglo-Catholics of a secure place in the Church of England. Instead, there is pressure being applied to Synod members to stand against any form of legal provision. A recent paper[29] published by WATCH and written by the Revd Canon Peggy Jackson[30] says that in order for women to trust the Church in upholding the (future) policies,

*'it follows that it will **no longer be appropriate to select, train and bring into ordained ministry** those who from the outset will have a conscientious objection to a central part of those policies – i.e. to the full and equal status of women and men together in holy orders'.*

The present draft proposals for the consecration of women bishops offer dissenters an assurance of a place in the Church of England with a Code of Practice. However, a Code of Practice simply offers a means of being nice to those traditionalists presently in the Church of England until they die out and until the doors of our theological colleges are shut to men and women who hold an authentic biblical position. This is discrimination; discrimination against anyone, men or women who are not uniformist!

---

[29] Women Bishops and the Protection of Integrity, March 2008
[30] Team Rector of Mortlake with East Sheen and Dean of Women's Ministry for Southwark Diocese (from June 2009 Archdeacon of Llandaff)

If in future people continue to approach the Bible with a Cultural, Revisionist mindset, it is quite feasible that they might in time try to explain away just about anything that offends them.

But for me this same Bible is a life-line to a greater understanding of God's perfect wisdom. Just as He directed the congregation (church) of Israel in the Wilderness, so it seems to me that we have sound teaching from the Old and New Testaments to direct the Church in this our day. That instruction need not, should not, be driven by the secular aspirations of a particular time in history but by the eternal word of Almighty God; however awkward or unpalatable that may be in modern society.

Do we not worship an omniscient God , the same yesterday, today and tomorrow? Is the outworking of our faith to follow after the secular fashion of our age or the eternal and timely teaching as manifested in the Lord Jesus Christ? No! Let us rid our minds of contemporary assumptions and go back to the biblical material to seek what the Holy Spirit is saying to us through it.

BIBLIOGRAPHY

•••••••••••••

Baker J (ed), Consecrated Women? Canterbury Press 2004

Benn W & Bray G, A Way Forward, ORTHOS, 2006

Beckwith R, Ovey M & Breckwoldt P, Women Bishops in the Church,
    Moulton Parish Church, England, a study booklet 2007

Burkhill M & Vibert S, Ministry Work Group Statement, Latimer Trust, LT1

Burkhill M, Why are there objections to women being bishops in the C of E? Reform

Burkhill M, Women's Ordination, Discussion Paper no. 2 Reform 1993

Church Society, Women Bishops? Understanding God's Will 2006

Ferguson S.B, Packer J.I, & Wright D.F, New Dictionary of Theology, IVP 1988

Gardener P, Ordination for Whom? ORTHOS, Occasional Paper no. 3

Grady J.L, 10 Lies the Church Tells Women, Charisma House 2000

Grudem W, Evangelical Feminism & Biblical Truth, IVP 2004

Grudem W, Systematic Theology, Zondervan 1994

Hunwicke J, Consecrated Women? A Comparison, Canterbury Press 2004

Hurley J, Man & Woman in Biblical Perspective, Zondervan 1981

Jackson P, Women Bishops and the Protection Of Integrity, WATCH 2008

Kassian, M, Women, Creation & the Fall, Crossways 1990

Lawler P, Dogged by the Collar? Discussion Paper no. 13, Reform

Matthews V, Surprised by Grace: An Episcopal Pilgrimage, SEARCH Vol.28, No.3, 2005

Nixson R, Liberating Women for the Gospel, Hodder & Stoughton 1997

Peterson D, Concerning the ministry of women in the church today

Piper J, & Grudem W, Recovering Biblical Manhood & Womanhood, Crossways 1991

Rigney J (ed), Women & the Episcopate, Affirming Catholicism 2006

Rushton J (ed), Twenty Questions on Women's Ordination Answered, Asc for the
    Apostolic Ministry

Ryrie C.C, Basic Theology, Victor Books 1988

Smith B, Walk This Way – Ephesians, Matthias Media 1996

Stott J, The Message of 1 Timothy & Titus, IVP 1996

Voltzenlogal, Women in the Ministry, Unpublished

JOURNALS & REPORTS

Giles Sheena, Woman Alive Magazine, February 2003

GRAS Newsletter Spring issue 2008

GRAS, The Scandal of the Blackburn Report, October 2001

GS Misc 826, Women in the Episcopate 2006

GS Misc 827, Resources for Reflection 2006

GS Misc 885, Women in the Episcopate? An Anglican – Roman Catholic dialogue 2008

Guildford Report, House of Bishops' Women Bishops Group, 2006

Kasper, Cardinal, Bishops' Meeting Address, 6 June 2006

Presentation to the Rochester Commission, Desiring what is true or Defending Desire?
    Reform 2001

Rochester Rpt, Women Bishops in the Church of England? Church House Pub. 2004

Shaw Jane, 'How Unlike God', Third Way Magazine Vol.24, No.8, November 2001

WATCH, Briefing Notes, January 2006

Wright N.T, & Stancliffe D, Women and Episcopacy - A Response to Cardinal Kasper,
    First Impression 2006

Grateful thanks are extended to the many people that in several ways have made this publication possible, especially The Anglican Association, Bible Truth Publishers, Reform and Various Church of England General Synod members.

Different views amongst Evangelicals concerning the role of women in the local church

EGALITARIAN LEFT	COMPLEMENTARIAN CENTRE		DOMINANT RIGHT
Galatians 3:28	1 Corinthians 11	1 Timothy 2	1 Corinthians 14
In Christ there is no male or female. Men and women have the same roles.	Women can pray and prophesy = preach. Only men can take charge of a church. Women can do everything else providing they are under male authority.	Women can not teach or exercise authority over men. Women can teach other women, teenagers and children.	Women should remain silent in church. Women have no public role.

On the Egalitarian left...

These people stress Galatians 3:28 - in Christ there is no male or female - and largely ignore the other passages or write them off as cultural. Women then end up doing almost exactly the same things as men.

On the dominant right...

Some stress 1 Corinthians 14: 34 - women should remain silent in the churches - so women have no public role. Anyone from a Brethren church background will have come across this view.

On the left of the complementarian centre...

These people emphasize 1 Corinthians 11 - women can pray and prophesy under authority - and allow women to preach occasionally, lead meetings, lead mixed Bible study groups etc.

On the right of the complementarian centre...

These people emphasize 1 Timothy 2 - I do not permit a woman to teach or have authority over a man - so women do not preach in the mixed gathering (but may be able to lead mixed Bible study groups).

This page included with grateful thanks to Revd Carrie Sandom.